ELLE DECOR
PORTFOLIOS

DECORATING
IDEAS

Cover: photos, top, left to right:
© Patrice Pascal, Barbara Bourgois; Guillaume de Laubier, Marie-Claire Blanckaert;
Patrice Pascal, Barbara Bourgois; Yutaka Yamamoto, Barbara Bourgois.
Bottom, left to right:
© Patrice Pascal, Barbara Bourgois; Joël Laiter, Barbara Bourgois.

Copyright © 2003 Filipacchi Publishing for the present edition

Copyright © 2002 Editions Filipacchi, Société SONODIP – *Elle Décoration*, for the French edition

Translated from French by Simon Pleasance and Fronza Woods
Copy edited by Jennifer Ditsler

ISBN: 2 85018 621 X

Color separation: HAFIBA

Printed and bound in Italy by Canale

DECORATING IDEAS

filipacchi
publishing

A home gets its personality from the ideas put into it, but the real refinement and uniqueness of a place is in the little details that go into its decorating. How do you go about creating an original setting by making your own curtains, screens or partitions? How can you repaint your walls and furniture in a way that is both clever and modern? What might you do with your old furnishings and knick knacks, with your photos and artworks?

Whether you are an amateur decorator or a professional, you will find in this book a number of helpful and creative solutions to these and many other interior decor questions. Solutions that don't require a special talent for wallpapering or painting, carpentry or framing, in order to take from these pages fresh ideas and pointers to decoration transformations that are practical and doable.

Decorating Ideas was written to share tricks of the decorating trade with you, and to help you create a personal style for your own interiors. With the help of ideas gleaned from these pages and several practical suggestions gathered together at the end of this book, you can turn your house or apartment into the space you've always dreamed of.

CONTENTS

CURTAINS

BETWEEN FASHION AND DECORATION, THERE ARE A THOUSAND WAYS TO DRESS A WINDOW. DOUBLE CURTAINS PLAY A GAME OF "NOW YOU SEE ME, NOW YOU DON'T." CURTAIN TOPS COME SMOCKED, RUFFLED OR WITH BOX OR PINCH PLEATS, AND TIEBACKS ADD THE FINISHING TOUCH OF ELEGANCE.

Left. Light, two-tone curtains made with a sky-blue fabric, combined with white cotton organdy. The play of transparency and opacity skillfully creates a striped effect.

Above. A wide curtain panel in a 100% cotton fabric with small box pleats to conceal the fastener for the hooks.

CURTAINS

Gathered then folded at regular intervals, these pleats are held in place above and below by a band of fabric sewn on horizontally. The curtain is attached with ribbons.

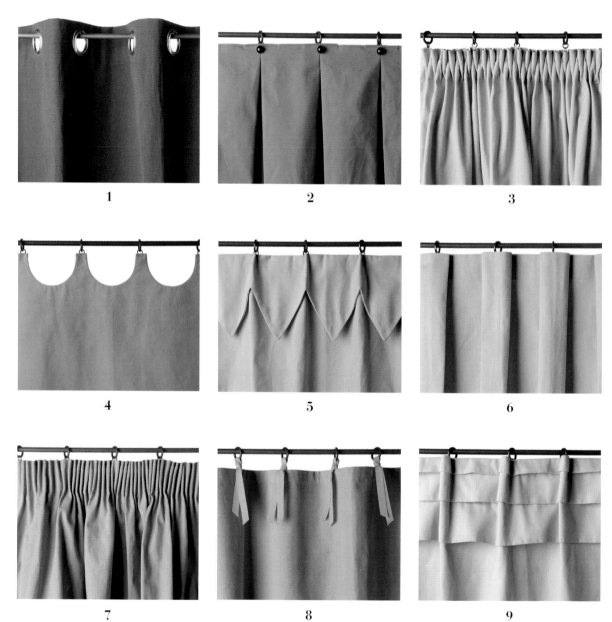

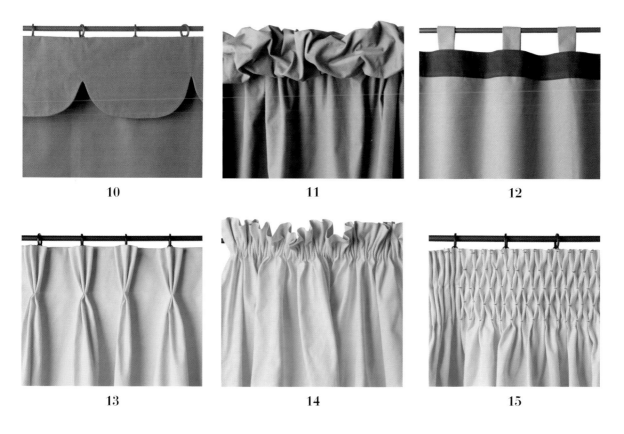

10

11

12

13

14

15

1. Grommets for hanging curtains. These make it possible to slip the curtain rod directly through the curtain.

2. Flat pleats held in place by a few stitches concealed under a button.

3. Curtain fitted on gathering tape and evenly gathered.

4. Scalloped cuts. 1/2 circle. hanging rings.

5. Pointed scalloped flaps with about 3/4-in. pleat for sewing on the fasteners.

6. Evenly spaced box pleats, held

in place in the middle by a fastener.

7. Fine pleats mounted on gathering tape and pulled together as tightly and closely as possible.

8. Straight hemmed curtain decorated with ribbons which serve as ties.

9. Decreasing 3 hered pinch pleat. pinched together at regular intervals to fix the fasteners.

10. Scalloped flaps and rings sewn without any folds.

11. Ruffled border effect created with just a wide hem and an extendable curtain rod.

12. Use of fabric in a contrasting color and tabs for curtain rings.

13. Three fold pinch pleat for a very sophisticated curtain.

14. Gathered very simply and slipped directly onto the curtain rod.

15. Meticulous smocking work mounted on gathering tape.

TIEBACKS

Left. Gold effects for a tieback that has been lined and trimmed with braid, the design is based on a Chinese silk embroidery. In the original, gold threads would have been used, but they are an expensive and tricky material to work with. Pearl cotton has been substituted instead which comes in several tones of shimmering gold and happens to be very well suited to the peony and lotus motifs used here. The tieback is very wide, solidly lined and trimmed with braid on the edge so it is sturdy enough to hold back a very heavy double curtain or drape. The embroidery on the left side is done in the reverse of the embroidery on the right side.

Above, right. This very simple tieback, made out of the same silk as the drape, is finished off by a triple flounced rosette with a button in the center.

Bottom, right. Here, the tieback has been made with the same fabric as the lining. Shaped like a banana, it is trimmed with a flat pleated flounce.

TIEBACKS

Above, left. Fashion designer Michel Klein's innovation: a braid lends its personality to the tieback.

Below, left. This tieback picks up the color of the drapes and the undercurtains. This tieback is made all the more elegant by its lovely tapered finishings.

Right. An armful of flowers for a tieback. Inspired by an 18th-century garland, a superb bit of topstitching on a high-quality white cotton makes this an exquisite tieback.

SHADES

WHETHER CONTEMPORARY SHADES MADE OF THIN SLATS, OR THE TRADITIONAL VERSION MADE OF RICE PAPER, BLINDS HAVE THE KNACK OF BRINGING ERAS AND STYLES TOGETHER IN A HARMONIOUS UNION. THEY DIVIDE UP THE SPACE, SHAPE AND REGULATE THE LIGHT, AND HELP CREATE ATMOSPHERE.

Left. Lined flat roman shades are finished with pointed edges and set off by trimmings in two shades of brick-red which pick up the color of the carpet.

Above. These unique ceiling shutters, covering a huge skylight, are made of limed wood that matches the walls.

SHADES

A great idea
realized at
Dominique
Kieffer's—
something old
becomes something
new by turning an
antique-style
curtain into a blind.
The shade is free,
requiring only
a rod at the
bottom of the
curtain-*cum*-shade
to show off the
pattern of the lace.

This cotton
Londonshade has
a loose finish to
create a light, soft
scroll effect. Roller
window shades are
fitted directly
onto the window.

21

SHADES

In fashion designer Kenzo's living room, which looks out onto the swimming pool, roller window shades have the finishing touch of little white pebbles attached to the ends of their pull cords— an unexpected, organic and very pretty finish.

François-Joseph
Graf designed
this soft roman
shade in white
fabric, edged with
a decorative cloth
tape, the same used
to cover the walls.

23

Opposite. Alternating taupe and sienna-colored linen on a round curtain rod, this elegant shade is reminiscent of colorful banners. For the three styles shown on these pages, see instructions on page 112.

Above, left. The ruffles
in this Austrian
shade in 100% linen
were created by tieing
strips of fabric together
at the bottom of
the shade.

Above, right.
This linen shade is a
variation of the style shown
on the left. To recreate it,
replace the ties with hemp
strings and sew each knot,
from top to bottom.

approximately 7 3/4 in.
from the edges and, at the
center, every 11 3/4 in.
Bring the ends of the string
together, two by two,
to create just the amount
of ruffle you want.

SHADES

Left. Blinds made of thin black slats accentuate the rounded contours of this window in Jacques Le Guennec's dining room. The resulting halo of light effect makes a perfect backdrop for two dramatic cactuses which have pride of place in their wood and straw planters. flanking a 19th-century table made of bamboo with finely worked ebony surface.

Right. Didier Gomez chose a modern combination of materials for his dressing room. Doors are fitted onto long. chrome-plated bars while walls and closets have a flecked maple-wood finish; a perfect match for the wooden blinds. The armchair was designed by Christian Liaigre.

SHADES

Left. A custom-made
Venetian blind.
The narrow wooden
slats can be mounted
on cord or braid.
Above, top.
Pleated, linen blinds.
Above, bottom.
Stained ramin blinds.

Above, top. Boat blind made
of 100% peacock-blue cotton.
Above, bottom. A custom-
made American shade, in
natural linen with a
"rising sun" motif.
Right. At Kenzo's, traditional
rice paper panels not only
define the space, but serve
as shades as well.

LAMPSHADES

IF YOU WANT A CLASSIC LOOK, TRY PLEATS OR WIDE STRIPES, BUT FOR SOMETHING MORE FANCIFUL, EXPERIMENT WITH DIFFERENT MOTIFS. WHEN IT COMES TO LAMPSHADES, ANYTHING GOES.

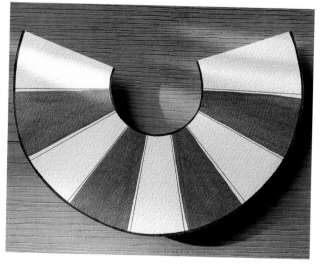

Left. These wide-striped lampshades were mounted on wooden candlestick holders. To make them: copy the pattern shown above (the rim and the stripes) onto watercolor paper. Cut the lampshade out and with gouache, paint every other stripe, as well as a very thin (little more than 1/8 in.-wide) border on the upper and lower rim of the lampshade, let dry. Apply glue to one of the end white stripes, put the other end on top of it and hold in place with paper clips, until the glue has dried thoroughly.

**For all the lampshades shown here and next spread,
see instructions on page 113.**

Below. Scalloped-edged lampshades made out of paper are
mounted on glass stands. The transparent quality
of the glass adds an interesting dimension.

Right. With a bit of stiff paper, it is easy to make these pretty
pleated lampshades. Here warm-toned paper dresses up
smooth-surfaced and fluted earthenware candlestick holders.

Following spread, left. Improvisation is the order of the day for these cut-out and pierced lampshades, and, as motifs go, the possibilities are as boundless as your imagination.

Following spread, right. And what if there was a lampshade for every day? Scalloped, gilded, pleated; they are festive, easy to make and full of wonderful, creative and colorful ideas.

PAINT

FOR A CHANGE OF DECOR WITHOUT TURNING THE OVERALL DESIGN
OF THE HOUSE UPSIDE DOWN, HERE ARE THE MOST COMMONLY
USED PAINTING TECHNIQUES TO ENABLE YOU TO ALTER THE LOOK
OF FLOORS, WALLS AND FURNITURE.

Left. To create this design, you need 4-in. wide
wooden slats laid together to form a 40 x 55-in.
rectangle (these are the dimensions of this
particular design, but the variations are infinite
based on the size of your room). Use the lightest
paint for the background and a deeper tone to
highlight the edge. After that, it's up to you to
coordinate your colors to create a signature design.

Above. From the classic paintbrush to the
ingenious streaking brush by way of sponges
and painter's knives, there are plenty of
instruments to help you give your walls the
most surprising effects. Here, a stucco
obtained from a ready-made preparation to
which natural sienna, orange and red oxide
pigments have been added.

sponge   spattered   cheesecloth   smoothed

rag   waxed   stucco   whisked

PAINT

Previous spread:

With a sponge

All surfaces can be worked
with a sponge—walls, ceilings.
floors, etc.— as long as they are
covered beforehand with a
plain-colored paint.

Spattered

This painting technique is quite
delicate but can be applied to
large as well as small objects.

With a cheesecloth

To obtain this effect, special
tools are required: a broad, flat
brush and several pieces of
cheesecloth with the four
corners folded over to form
round pads.

Smoothed

The smoothed effect comes from
imitation-wood techniques used
in the mid-18th century.

With rags

Painting using pieces of cloth
or rags is practical, quick and
easy to do, and doesn't require
any special tools. It can be
applied to walls, floors and
furniture.

Waxed

This is the simplest technique
of all. Apply satin-finish paint
to walls. Leave to dry. Then
spread a virgin wax over them
using another brush.

Stucco

The stucco mixture is sold
ready-made in white so
you can add any color pigment
you desire. Then, using a
painter's knife, apply the
preparation in small strokes,
a bit like rendering. Smooth it
on lightly or heavily, depending

on the effect you prefer.
Here, ultramarine and black
pigments have been added to a
ready-made stucco.

Whisked

This finish derives straight from
the imitation-oak decorative
technique.

Opposite. Creating the illusion
of old paneling on a brand
new wall is something even
budding do-it-yourselfers can
do. A clever trick to give some
soul and character to a room.

(For all these techniques,
see instructions on
pages 114-115.)

Creating beautiful doors and walls with paint.

Below. To achieve this shading effect on your walls, use a white, matte acrylic paint for the undercoat and yellow ochre for the second coat, applied with a short-handled household brush. Once the color coat is dry, make a finish consisting of the two colors and water. The final effect is created by wiping a cloth over the wall to shade any lines that are too hard.

Below. The effect of vertical stripes for the walls is also created using matte acrylic paint, in beige and brown hues. The beige is applied first with a roller to create the background. Once this coat has dried, dip a rice-straw broom in the brown paint being careful to paint straight from ceiling to floor to create the stripes. The doors are made with 30 mm, half-round strips held in place by small brads. A bright red and black satin-finish paint has been chosen here.

PAINT

To produce this well accentuated, sponge-painted checkerboard pattern, cover a wall with 12-in. wide fir planks. First apply an undercoat of well-diluted paint to obtain a very pale background, making sure that this coat is good and dry before continuing. To obtain the final effect, cut a synthetic sponge into a square and glue to a piece of plywood cut to its size, on which a small brace has been previously glued to create a handle. Dip the sponge into the paint and scrape off the excess with a spatula so it can be applied evenly to the wooden wall, to obtain the checkerboard design.

FURNITURE
TO PAINT

BE THEY BARGAINS FOUND AT AUCTION OR AT A SECONDHAND STORE,
OR ITEMS UNEARTHED IN THE DEPTHS OF AN ATTIC, OLD FURNITURE
FINDS A NEW PERSONALITY ONCE IT HAS BEEN STRIPPED AND
REPAINTED. PICTURED HERE ARE SOME EXAMPLES OF THESE MOTH-TO-
BUTTERFLY TRANSFORMATIONS.

Left. Odds and ends: Furniture from an attic before being "salvaged." From left to right: a chest of drawers, an old office armchair, a butcher-block table with broken feet, old bistro chairs, a frame, a screen without its fabric and an old-fashioned Henri II overmantel.

Opposite. The chest of drawers is made of wood with a well-defined grain: perfect for an elegant green varnish that leaves the wood grain visible. New drawer handles complete the restored version of this piece.

Left. This butcher-block table has found new life as a spruced-up sideboard. Its legs were partly worm-eaten, but with an inch or two sawed off the bottom, it's right back on its feet. After replacing the top and using a plank to block the gap left by a missing drawer. Basque-red paint provides the finishing touch to give this table pride of place in the kitchen.

Right. Unearthed in an attic, all that was left of this screen was its frame. The panels were remade in standard deck-chair fabric, and simply stapled (although you can also glue or nail them). The frame was painted a pretty moss green that harmonizes with the natural hue of the fabric.

FURNITURE

Left. Installed behind the sink, the Henri II overmantel with its elegant bevelled mirror becomes the focal point of the bathroom. Its pearl-gray cabled columns standing out against a white painted background bring this classic piece beautifully up to date. It was necessary to strip off the original paint and apply several coats of new paint to smooth out all the flaws in the wood.

Right. Painted in two colors, the bistro chairs are now both modern and stylish. The rush-blue and satin-finish white used on the chair backs produce an unexpected effect that was inexpensive and easy to achieve.

SLIPCOVERS

ANY COUCH CAN BE EASILY TRANSFORMED FOR A LOOK THAT SUITS YOUR STYLE. ELEGANT, DRAMATIC OR SIMPLY COVERED IN NATURAL FABRICS, THE OPTIONS ARE ENDLESS. THE ART OF JUGGLING FABRICS TO CREATE SEAT AND ARMCHAIR COVERS TAKES ON MANY FORMS HERE WITH YOUR IMAGINATION AS YOUR GUIDE.

Left. Five khaki-colored army blankets found in a Paris flea market cover these simple sofas. The cushion covers are brightened up with a 2 in.-wide red satin braid.
Above. A trick for giving footstools a unique look: make small plaid blankets to lay over each stool. Here, both a red and a twine-colored plaid have been fringed with imitation suede and criss-crossed with flax thread. (See instructions on page 115.)

Below. Simplicity and raw
material are elemental for
this 100% linen slipcover,
enhanced by a thin linen
braid and two cushions covered
with a cotton and linen fabric.

Below. A more sophisticated
way to dress your sofa:
this slipcover with box
pleats. tied on the sides.
The fabric is cotton with
a chevron design.

ONE SOFA, THREE IDEAS

**One bed base +
One mattress =
Three sofa ideas.**
With a little care and
imagination it is easy
to implement your own
ideas. Using a single mattress,
and divans which, once
they have their covers
removed, can be turned into
comfortable, spare beds.

Opposite. To make a back
for this couch, a rod cleverly
keeps the cushions in place.
The mattress slipcover is made
to imitate the look of
old woolen mattresses.
(See instructions on page 116.)

ONE SOFA, THREE IDEAS

Above. Covered and piped headboards become arms for this sofa which uses an antiqued linen fabric in an interplay of three colors: black, brown and rust. The top of the bed is also piped, and the fabric over its base is enhanced by a box pleat in the middle. The cushion covers are treated like pillowcases in a mixture of the same fabric, but in different shades.

Above. The soft, padded effect of the upholstery gives this sofa a comfortable look. To ensure that the fabric is stretched tight over the top of the bed and over the three cushions forming the back, use a Polyfil padding fabric. then apply the fabric, topstitch it in 6-in. lozenge shapes and pipe the edges. The smaller cushions are buttoned at the center and piped. On the bed base, the fabric is decorated with box pleats at the center and at each end.

59

CHAIRS

Left. An original method for covering chairs: Using a pure cotton fabric, these knotted slipcovers look like very stylish petticoats!

Right.
A footstool elegantly decorated at each corner and covered with 100% cotton fabric held in place by coordinating ties and finished off with a tassel at each leg.

One armchair, two slipcover ideas

Made of floral cotton, the elegant and cozy comfort of Persian boudoir is evoked in this fabric, a reproduction of original 18th-century drawings printed in a range of old-style hues. This pure cotton fabric is fashioned into box pleats held in place from behind by two bows which match the colors in the printed fabric.

ARMCHAIRS

These durable cotton ticking fabrics fit equally well
in a seaside setting as they do in a rustic or urban
environment. With an affinity for simple and relaxed
atmospheres, stripes go well with the geometry of checks
and tartans. This slipcover is held in place from behind
by two bows in the same 100% cotton fabric.

KILIMS

Hailing from Persia, Turkey and Afghanistan, ancient or contemporary kilims are in fashion. They make superb cushions, wall hangings, rugs and tapestries. You can find their patterns and colors printed on all sorts of fabrics. Usually inspired from nature with geometric designs of stylized flowers, trees and leaves, the kilim decor goes very well with the most varied interiors.

Above. An unusual mixture of leather and kilim fabric.
Below. Oriental inspiration for this ottoman made of two foam cushions joined together by four braided loops. It is covered with a kilim-style cotton fabric.
Right. Old kilims reused on period Swedish chairs.

REPRODUCTIONS

TO MAKE REPRODUCTION FURNITURE LOOK LESS CONVENTIONAL, OR TO REVIVE OLD CHAIRS LONG AGO FORGOTTEN IN THE DEPTHS OF AN ATTIC, THE SKY IS THE LIMIT. PAIR BRIGHT PAINTS WITH UNEXPECTED FABRICS AND PLAY WITH THE DELIGHTFULLY DARING CONTRASTS BETWEEN TODAY'S HIGH-TECH FABRICS AND YESTERYEAR'S LOUIS XVI CHAIR.

Left. Natural wood chair frames perform an acrobatic act before undergoing transformation shown on the next few pages. These chairs were manufactured by the Coulombs furniture factory in France and are sold ready to be upholstered.

Opposite. A Louis XIV chair with Venetian influences. This rustic chair was restored to current tastes with a black enamel—similar to those used on Venetian gondolas—to enhance its ornate carvings and rid it of its formalism.

Left. A rustic wing chair bedecked as if for the opera. A glamorous red clads this Provençal armchair: its discreet design is instantly transformed by the simple choice of a bright fabric. While elegant, the chair is welcoming and comfortable and will very soon find its place at the fireside.

Below. Avant-garde Regency—a real stunner! Treated in matching tones, as here with a preference for direct, bright, dynamic colors (you could also imagine it in bright yellow or royal blue), this Regency armchair, rejuvenated with a dash of daring, will instantly enliven the most stately of settings.

Below. These days, it is encouraged to turn your bathroom into a movie star's dream. The softness of terry cloth combined with the refinement of a bold monogram adorn this elegant Louis XVI-style chair. The chair is painted in satin-finish white for a white-on-white effect.

Right. An interpretation of the Louis XVI style in the Art Deco spirit. The powerful personality of an Art Deco-inspired fabric lends plenty of character to this wing chair, where the painted wood borrows one of the bright colors of the modern mosaic covering the chair.

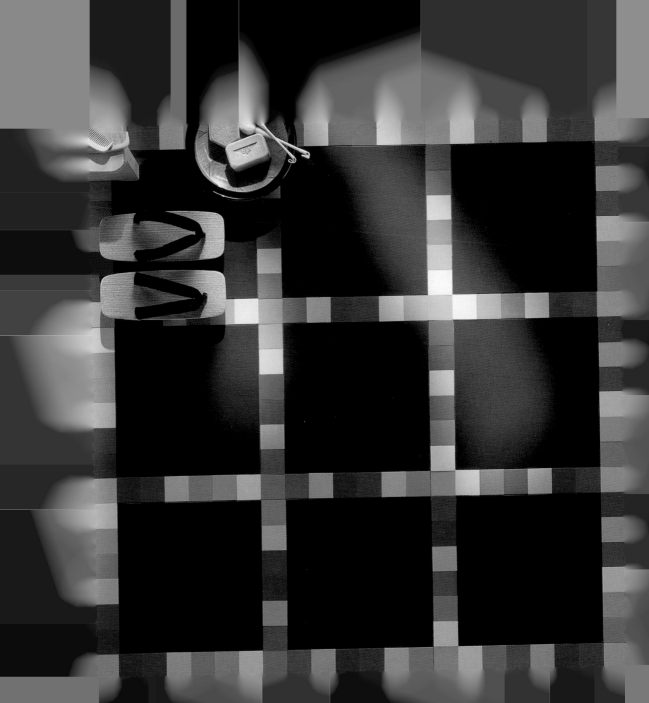

FLOORS

THERE IS NO SHORTAGE OF VARIATIONS WHEN IT COMES TO INVENTING DESIGNS FOR FLOORS. FROM FLIRTING WITH MATTE, GLOSSY, FLECKED OR PLAIN STONEWARE TILES TO MAKING YOUR OWN RUGS TO MATCH THE DECORATION OF YOUR HOME, THERE ARE COUNTLESS POSSIBILITIES AVAILABLE TO EVERYONE TO SET THE TONE FOR EACH AND EVERY ROOM.

Left. The contrast of matte and gloss lends relief to this floor made with polished ceramic stoneware tiles in 12 x 12 in., and smaller 2 x 2 in. squares. **Above.** An assortment of ceramic tiles, in matte and polished finishes. Ceramic tiles have long been used in commercial buildings due to their durability and low cost.

You can do it yourself or design the pattern you want and hire a professional craftsman to lay it. For those who would like to do it themselves, use a base of fresh cement or ready-made cement glue which is spread with a serrated spatula. These tiles are easy to cut with a special tool available in all specialized stores.

FLOORS

Above. The Provençal design of this kitchen floor was made with 4 x 4-in. tiles in alternating rows of diamond and square shapes with small multi-colored 1 x 1-in. square tiles placed in between to create a carpet-like effect.

Opposite. This bathroom floor with its subdued pattern combines black (8 x 8-in. tiles) with flecked blue-green (2 x 2-in. tiles). To create a warmer feeling, you can play with beiges, brick reds and browns.

Herringbone or diamond-shaped, plain or striped carpets, here you have a stylistic exercise for covering your stairs. All these models are made of woven wool with herringbone or striped patterns, except for the carpet shown on the right which is in sisal trimmed with braid.

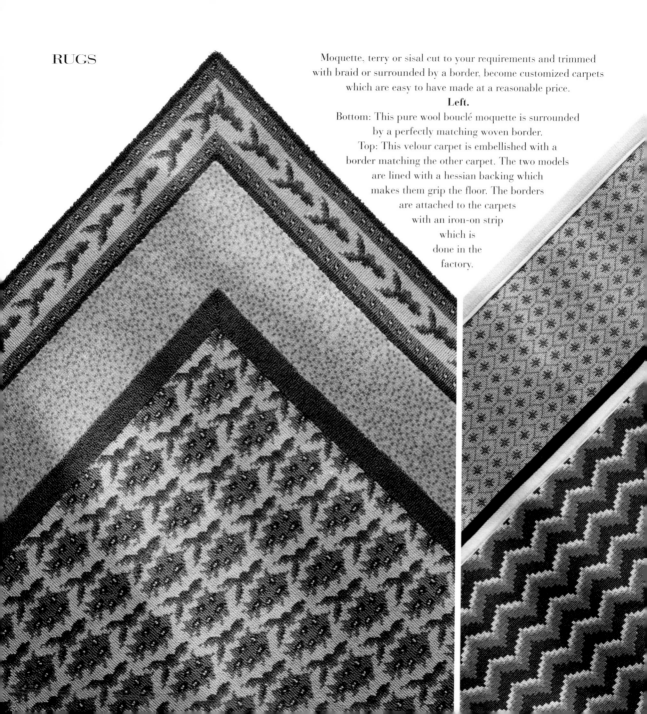

RUGS

Moquette, terry or sisal cut to your requirements and trimmed with braid or surrounded by a border, become customized carpets which are easy to have made at a reasonable price.

Left.

Bottom: This pure wool bouclé moquette is surrounded by a perfectly matching woven border.

Top: This velour carpet is embellished with a border matching the other carpet. The two models are lined with a hessian backing which makes them grip the floor. The borders are attached to the carpets with an iron-on strip which is done in the factory.

Middle.
Two cotton terry carpets hemmed with braid.
For the bottom model, the carpet braid is double stitched;
for the top one, it is stitched on the bias.

Right.
Top: This herringbone-patterned carpet is made of natural
jute surrounded by a double braid overlaid on linen and
machine stitched. Bottom: Made with multi-colored
coir, it is edged with a dyed linen braid.
The whole carpet is machine stitched
and affixed to a latex backing
which prevents it from
slipping and holds
the carpet's
shape.

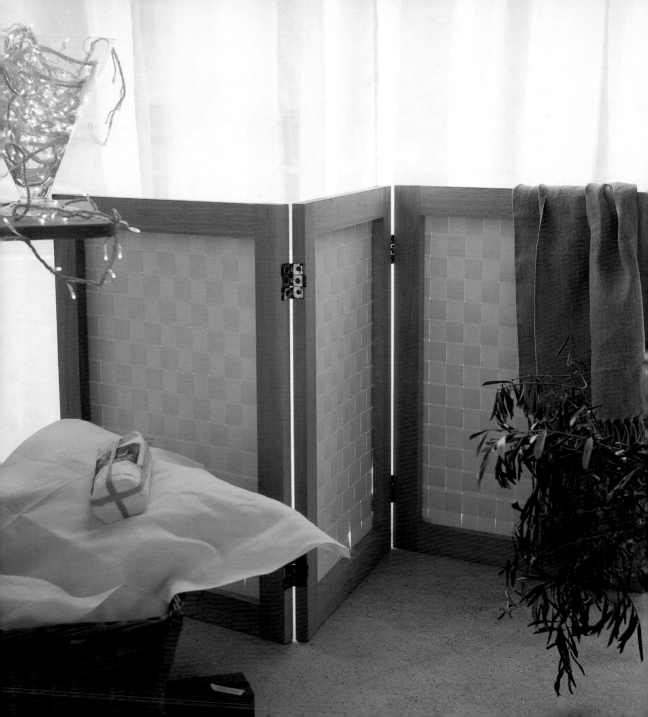

SCREENS

PRACTICAL AND AESTHETICALLY PLEASING, SCREENS AND PARTITIONS MAKE IT POSSIBLE—SIMPLY AND IMPERMANENTLY—TO ALTER THE PHYSICAL ASPECT OF AN APARTMENT BY CREATING SEPARATE SPACES OR "NOOKS." AND, AS IF BY MAGIC, MAKING BIG AND SMALL MESSES DISAPPEAR.

Left. This screen is made of woven strips of super royal-format white and ecru-colored paper. (See instructions on page 116.) **Above.** This padded model, made with two boards (3 x 2 ft., approx.) a pretty, plain chintz, golden hinges and carpet tacks, creates a warm and original atmosphere. The studwork is done on nicked lengths of metal strips covered with the same chintz.

Left. A clever way of lending style to simple reproductions: This 1940s-style wooden three-paneled screen is not difficult to make. (See instructions on page 117.)

Above. Screens are often used for hiding things. here. however. we see that they are also perfect for displaying things. This mahogany "photo screen" acts as a souvenir album.

Above. An Indian screen in lacquered wooden tracery is made of two adjoining screens (each leaf measures 48 x 15 in.) and has been sprayed with high gloss white paint for maximum effect.

Right. The wooden model pictured here, at once elegant and spare, is painted with a cream-colored enamel. Using special concealed hinges, it consists of four shutters each measuring 66 x 24 in.

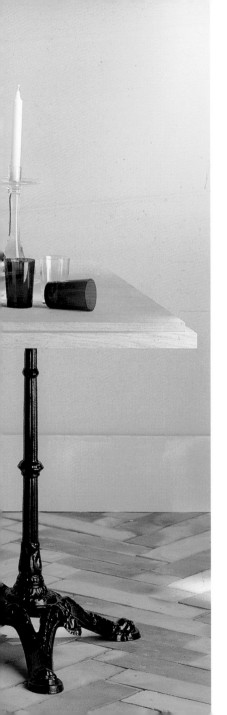

TABLE
LEGS AND
TOPS

THE ART OF TURNING PEDESTAL SINKS AND OCCASIONAL TABLES INTO SIDEBOARDS, TABLES AND CONSOLES: LOTS OF IDEAS FOR UNUSUAL CREATIONS DESIGNED FOR HOUSE AND GARDEN ALIKE.

Left. A simple and original creation: A table set on pedestals, the number of legs depends upon the desired length of the tabletop. These pedestals are new but you can easily find old ones in antique stores and flea markets, which may require stripping. If the table is intended for outdoor use, you must first apply an anti-rust product before painting the legs, and if the tabletop is wood, it must be painted. A marble top simplifies things since it works indoors and out. You can make a mock molding around the edge of the tabletop by nailing a wooden frame which will also hide the unsightly thickness of the hardware.

Left. Made from part of a Directoire-style balcony railing,
this console table is as handy inside as it is in the
garden, provided that the top is suitable for bad weather
(stone, marble, etc.), and as long as the stand is rust-proofed.
(See instructions on page 117.)

Center. Another idea for a console table:
An early 20th-century washstand in gilded brass
has a modern look fitted with a marble or
frosted glass top. This top is in oak varnished
with a mixed black and brown wash, and then waxed.

If the stand is not in good condition,
you can have it regilded or rechromed
by a specialist, to be found among restorers,
scrap metal dealers and certain antiques dealers.

Right. An improvised table using a 1930s pedestal sink
(basin removed). With a stone or marble top, this piece
also looks great in a garden. These pedestals can easily
be found in flea markets or architectural artifacts shops.

TABLETOPS

An original way of creating one-of-a-kind tables. For each model, the basic principle is the same: on a marine ply base (not affected by humidity), fit a top made of wood and tiles and surrounded by a border with glued corners. An 18th-century-style Provençal stand in wrought-iron treated in the "gun barrel" manner acts as the support.

Below, left. This oak and tile table is strong enough to be used in the house or in the garden. Because the assembly requires wooden parts that fit very precisely, it is better to have them prepared by a carpenter. The top is made of pieces of oak with pointed ends which fit snugly together. Between them are placed 8 x 8-in. cement tiles like a

checkerboard. An oak molding is fitted all around. The wood may be waxed or varnished.

Below, right. This all oak table, designed to resemble parquet, consists of slats fixed to a sheet of plywood and surrounded by a frame of the same wood, slightly bevelled. On the tabletop large identical squares were drawn in pencil, perpendicular to the grain of the wood with their edges slightly hollowed out with a saw, thus giving it the look of an inlay. Then the squares were painted (just one coat), with a matte paint which lets the wood show through. The table may either keep its rough look or be finished with a clear varnish.

Below. This tiled top combines plain tiles with small geometric shapes: It has a very graphic line, with its top of bright white ceramics, but its "dynamic" look is attained by a frieze of broken tiles forming a mosaic. It is finished by a black painted steel flange. The tiles measure 4 x 4 in.

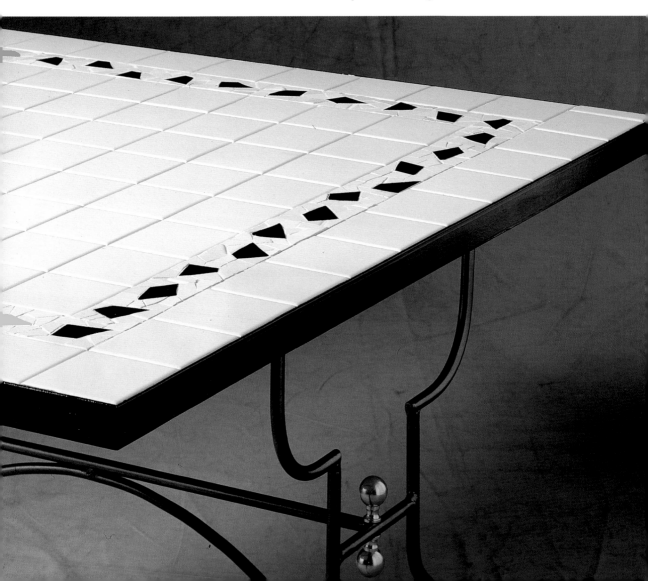

Below. Alternating plain tiles and patterns, this pretty sage-green table is simple to make. In the central section, tiles (8 x 8 in.) forming a geometric design are set off by a plain border. The edge of the tabletop is made with a wooden batten painted a satin-finish creamy white.

FRAMES
AND STANDS

DESIGNING AND ASSEMBLING YOUR OWN WORK OF ART BY
SELECTING ILLUSTRATIONS, PHOTOGRAPHS AND REPRODUCTIONS;
DISPLAYING VALUABLE OBJECTS AND TRAVEL SOUVENIRS. NOW YOU
CAN DO IT YOURSELF, THANKS TO A FEW CLEVER IDEAS.

Left. The multiple-
frame, jumble
principle combined
with a photo
frame makes
selected moments
captured on film
even more special.
(See instructions
on page 117.)

Opposite.
A changeable board
of botanical plates
found in second-
hand bookstores.
Ribbons nailed
at right angles
and diagonally
help keep the
prints in place.

FRAMES

Top, left. Halfway between frame and art object, a standing frame made of natural beech. (See instructions on page 118.)
Below. This horizontal frame is made of 2 lengths of round wooden beadboard, 12 pieces of non-reflecting glass and 2 lengths of wire. (See instructions on page 118.)
Right. This oak frame, in which you can fit several photos, looks like a window with small panes. To be made by a carpenter.

Left. This shimmering frame was made with a piece of velvet stretched over a wooden panel. For the frame itself, strips of black wooden beading have been used. The middle consists of a square of wood cut out and painted black, and fixed to the frame. A drawing or photo is then glued to it.

Opposite. A multiple frame: On a lathed wood panel with satin-finish red paint, four identical small panels are affixed, and covered with three kinds of black folded paper. The reproductions are then set in the middle.

FRAMES

Above. A frame within a frame. An oval frame is fixed to a rectangular, lathed wood panel painted with a satin finish.

Opposite. To make this covered frame, stretch a piece of natural linen over a wooden board. A smaller frame, made in the same way, is then affixed in the middle to hold the reproduction which you glue to it.

Right. A surprising marriage of colors and materials make up this tortoiseshell-like frame. It combines wood, tortoiseshell-patterned paper and aluminum strips. (See instructions on page 119.)

FRAMES

Right. These souvenir frames are made with sheets of cardboard in gray, silver and white. It's child's play to put together, creating a sophisticated and original result. (See instructions on page 119.)

Above. These undressed wooden frames creating a nest effect have simply been painted with enamel.

Opposite. A beechwood jigsaw-puzzle frame, painted blueish-gray is put together in four parts, two identical widths and two identical heights, with dovetail joints. Just fit the top and bottom to the two side pieces.

Below. Christian Astuguevieille's passion for natural things and *Art Brut* is clearly evident in his small study where he has installed a collection of mainly African insects.

Left. He uses this same boxing technique to display on the desk a leather bracelet called "the lobster," which he created himself. In the foreground, the throne chair made of painted rope is also one of his creations.

Below. An ingenious way of remembering important moments. Each composition is set under glass in a whitewashed wooden frame: all hail from different parts of the world.

Top row, from left to right: A mixture of seashells on a bed of sand (Philippines). An American-Indian headdress from the Amazon with parrot and eagle feathers (Brazil).

Paper necklaces, tiger balm and a sari blouse (India). Bottom row, from left to right: A mixture of Mao badges, combs, slipper, armband and new and old necklaces (China). A squaw doll and bone necklaces (North America). Beetles neatly arrayed above jackal heads which are part of a game called "Hippopotamus" (Egypt).

Below. All these small objects are placed, glued or pinned in black frames.
Top row, from left to right: A gaggle of bottle brushes. An abstract design using orange and white lentils. A line of wooden brushes.

Krug champagne labels.
Bottom row, from left to right: A mixture of cinnamon sticks and cloves. Wine labels. Chinese noodles in sheaves. Wine corks.

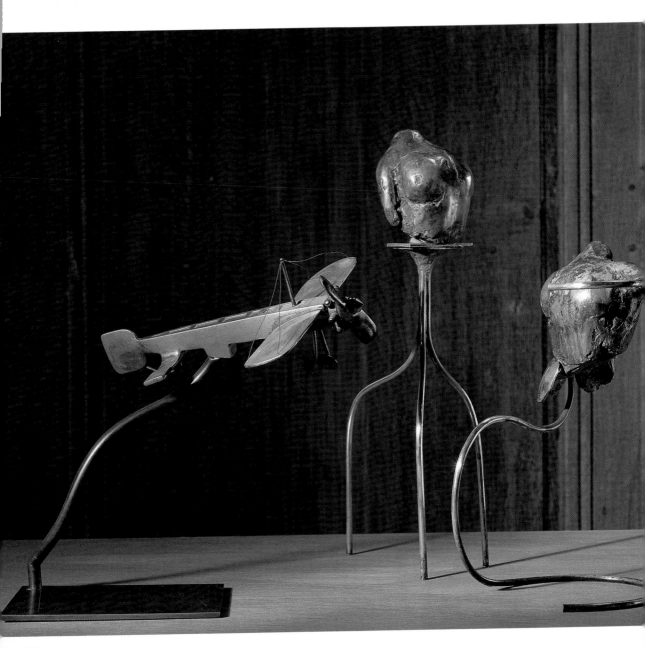

STANDS

An original way of
displaying
sculptures and
paintings and a few
ideas for stands,
pedestals and legs,
attractive and rich
in character.

Left. Designed by
the painter and
sculptor Charles
Matton, these
sinuous, silver
stands accentuate
two of his works
in unexpected
ways: "Torso" and
"Seated Woman."
The stand made
of patinated bronze
was created by the
Christian de
Beaumont
workshop to
display a 1930s
style airplane.

Right. This tall
stand is quite easy
to make with rods
of acid-patinated
iron. A seated
woman, by Philippe
Anthonioz, seems
to levitate atop it.

STANDS

Left to right. This tri-footed bronze stand has a witty quality and is easy to make yourself; bearing a shoetree, this was a present from Sarah Moon to Charles Matton.

When unfolded, a folding cross bar easel made of pear wood, created by Jeanine Roset for the Louvre line, measures 15 x 12-in. high, and when folded, 15 x 2-in. high.

This small wooden column, turned like ebony (10-in. high) and its patinated bronze base display a Chinese sphere.

A tripod (11-in. high) is original and easy to make. This example, in patinated bronze topped by a street gas cover displays a plaster bust by Philippe Anthonioz (10-in. high).

A unique piece, this stand of painted iron was manufactured by a locksmith. Designed not to be seen, these stirrup-like clasps hold an Amazon Indian headdress.

This adjustable reading light in brushed and varnished polished brass is 22-in. high and 10-in. wide; the stand measures 6 x 6-in.

Adjustable column stand and tripod in bronze. This patinated bronze stand (3 x 3 x 8-in. high) displays a hunting decoy.

Practical instructions

SHADES

TWO-COLOR SCHEME, PAGE 24
Supplies:
100% linen fabric in
two colors (the dimensions
given include the seams);
Upper strip: the width
of the window by 24-in. high.
Panel: the height of the
window by 12-in. wide.
Ties: 1-2-in. wide. Wadding:
make rolls just under 12-in.
wide by 1-in. diameter.
Fold the strip in two,
lengthwise. Side by side,
fit in the panels by

alternating the colors,
then place the ties,
one in front and one
behind, in the middle
of each panel. Sew the
thicknesses thus obtained
where the strip is joined.
Leave the sides free to insert
a round curtain rod.
At the bottom of each panel
make a 1-in. hem and slide
in the rolls of wadding.
Install the blind, roll down
and knot with the ties.

IN LINEN, PAGE 25 LEFT
Supplies:
Colored fabric, 100%
linen and white fabric;
self-adhesive Velcro
the width of the blind;
wooden batten the width
of the window; glue.
Cut the fabric to the
dimension of the window,
adding 1/2 inch on each side
(tucked in) and 2 in.
lengthwise (a 1-in.
hem top and bottom).
Machine sew all around.
To make the ties:
cut the white fabric into
4 strips bevelled on just

one side to the height
of the blind and 2-in.
wide (finished dimensions).
Make a knot in the
middle of each tie.
Sew at 8 in. from the
edges of the right part of
each of the strips, at the
top of the blind, back and
front. Affix half the Velcro
to the top of the blind.
Place the wooden batten
12 in. above the window,
glue the other half of the
Velcro above and fix the
blind to it. Knot the strips
to form the ruffle.

IN LINEN, PAGE 25 RIGHT
Supplies:
100% linen fabric;
18 lengths of hemp twine,
20 in. each, self-adhesive
Velcro the width of the blind,
wooden batten the width
of the window.
Proceed as for the
previous blind, replacing
the ties with the twine.
When you have finished,
join the lengths of twine,
two by two, to obtain
the desired ruffles.

LAMPSHADES

WITH SCALLOPED EDGES, PAGE 32

Supplies:
Watercolor paper, scissors, glue, needle, pencil.
Draw the lampshade on the back of the paper, broad at the bottom and narrow at the top and as straight. Using the needle, make small holes about 1/4 in. from the edges, following the shape of the scallop. Cut out the shade and join the ends with glue.

PLEATED, PAGE 33

Supplies:
Stiff, plain-colored paper, a large needle, thread, ruler, scissors, paper glue, pencil.
On the paper make a rectangle corresponding to the desired height and the lower circumference of the shade multiplied by three. (Example: for a cone that is 4-in. high with a finished circumference of 20 in., you will need a rectangle of 4 x 60 in.). Cut out. On the back of the long sides of the rectangle, make pencil marks every 1/2 in., neatly aligned. Make holes in the paper at these places, so as not to have to reproduce the marks on the outer side of the shade. Pleat the paper, making it fit accurately with the upper and lower marks. Flatten each pleat by smoothing with a ruler. Put the two ends together with glue to make a tubular shape. Let dry.

Thread the large needle with the yarn of your choice. Pass the needle into the pleats 1/2 in. from the upper edge of the shade, then pull to assemble the pleats.

CUT OUT OR PIERCED MODELS, PAGE 34

Supplies:
Stiff, plain-colored paper, backing paper, large needle, craft knife, paper glue, pencil.
Using a fine pencil, draw the leaves on the back of the stiff paper, as well as the edges (either straight or scalloped). Cut out the shade and the leaf motifs (starting from their tips and ending the cut just before reaching the ends in order to not completely detach them from the paper). Line the inside of the shade with backing paper to prevent direct glare from the bulb through the slits. For hens and stripes: pierce the motifs with a large needle. Glue the sides together.

WALL PAINTING

PAGES 38-39

The glaze:
Each wall painting technique makes use of a specific preparation which is called a glaze. To make this, mix petrol, linseed oil, a siccative, zinc oxide and color. This translucent preparation dries more slowly than a normal paint.

Sponge finish:
Make a monochrome glaze. Apply it with the help of a natural sponge. At the end of each session, wash the sponge with solvent then with soapy water and, finally, rinse it in clean water. You'll have to dampen it before using it again. Here, on a white background, a white, orange and chrome-colored glaze.

Spattered:
A round, pig-bristle brush will help to make this effect. Once the brush is filled with color, its handle is struck against a rod in order to spatter the paint on the surface. Beware: this operation is not easy. The further you are from the surface to be spattered, the bigger the patches of color. To obtain this effect on small objects, tap the brush against a finger and you will have greater control. The paint should be relatively liquid. Here, on a white background, matte black and white paint, then spattered white paint.

Cheesecloth finish:
With a broad, flat brush, apply a thin coat of glaze in every direction. Take a square of cheesecloth, fold in the four corners to form a round pad with which you remove part of the paint with a series of quick dabs. Change the pad as soon as it is too soaked. Here, on a white background, a black, chrome, natural umber and white glaze.

Smoothed:
Using a brush, vertically apply a thick oil-based glaze. Highlight the vertical lines with a streaking brush. To smooth the surface, you can use cloths or brushes depending on the effect you are after. Here, a first coat of two lighter colors has been applied to avoid too great a contrast between the background and the stripes. The background is orange

and white, and the finish
has been achieved by
sanding with sandpaper.

Cloth/rag finish

Over the undercoat, apply
the glaze with an ordinary
paintbrush—the glaze must
always be darker than the
background. Working
quickly, partly remove the
glaze before it is dry.
This operation is made
easier if it is done by two
people, one applying the
glaze, the other immediately
giving it the cloth finish
effect. Here, on a white
background, English green,
black, natural umber
and white glaze.

Whisked finish:

Apply a slightly thick end
glaze over the background,
smooth it off and then whisk
it with a special, long-
bristled brush. Be careful: if
the glaze is too liquid, the
whisking will give an effect
that is too "frenzied." Here,
on a white background, a
black and white glaze.

Giving the illusion
of aged paneling:

First apply a coat
of varnish on the paneling
to make it darker.
Let dry, then using
a small brush, unevenly
apply dabs of
wax which you will then
spread with your fingers.
After a 12-hour drying
period, apply a generous
coat of sky-blue paint
with a paintbrush, but
without pressing too hard
so as to not remove the wax.
Leave to dry for an entire
day. Then, with a cloth,
rub the parts where
the wax has been applied.
The paint will not have
stuck here, and the
varnished wood will
reappear in patches.
With a scraper, blur
the edges a little. Then
sand with fine-grained
sandpaper. Next, apply
the well-diluted sky-blue
paint to the uncovered
parts. Finally, paint
the upper section of
the wall a cream color.

FOOTSTOOLS

DO-IT-YOURSELF, PAGE 53
Supplies for a 16 x 16-in.
footstool:
28 in. of fabric, 57 in. wide,
28 in. of brushed cotton,
9 1/2 ft. of suedette fringes,
2 in.-wide, flax thread,
a large needle, tailor's chalk,
scissors.
Cut two 28 in. squares
in the fabric, and
in the brushed cotton a
very slightly smaller
square. Place the brushed
cotton in the middle of
the two squares of fabric,
then fit the suedette fringes

all around between the two pieces of fabric. Machine sew all four sides. Using the chalk, draw a grid in which each square is 5 1/2 x 5 1/2 in. Thread the needle with the flax and make 1-in. stitches on the grid, spaced 2 in. apart, taking in all the layers.

SOFAS

SOFA BED, PAGES 56-57
Supplies:
1 bed base, 1 twin mattress, 1 piece of foam-rubber

at least 1-in. thick, and cut the same size as the bed, rosettes, 1 length of piping, 1/2 in. in diameter, fabric for making the slipcover, cushions and covering the base, brass rod and fixtures.
On the seat side, slide the foam-rubber under the slipcover, and hold it in place with the rosettes, giving the effect of padding. Run the piping around the mattress, top and bottom. Cover the square legs and bed base with the same fabric, pad the cushions the

same way as the mattress with five rosettes. On the back of the cushions, make three tabs through which the rod will then be slipped. Fix the rod to the wall.

SCREENS

BEIGE SCREEN, PAGE 80
Supplies:
3 sheets of white paper and 3 sheets of ecru paper, super royal format, minimum 90 lbs, 3 oak frames measuring 22 x 30 x 2 in., 4 hinges, scissors, glue.
Assemble the three frames using the hinges. Cut out the white sheets of paper lengthwise in strips of 2 in. plus a 1 in. rim (which will be affixed to the frame). In the ecru sheets, cut 2 in. strips running widthwise. Then weave these strips one by one together with the white sheets. Once you have finished the weaving, glue or nail each sheet to the back of the frame.

**1940S-STYLE SCREEN,
PAGE 82**

Supplies:
3 wooden panels,
3 wooden frames 3-in. wide,
diluted white paint,
3 sheets of wood for
each panel, black glaze,
oil paint obtained by mixing
crimson, black and burnt
sienna, plaster stars, glue.
On each panel glue a
3-in. wide wooden frame.
Paint it with the diluted
white paint. Inside each
frame fix a sheet
of wood to be covered
with black glaze.
Then stick the plaster
stars around the frames.

CONSOLE

**CONSOLE,
PAGE 88, LEFT**

Supplies:
A length of balcony railing
to be found at a scrap
metal dealer or restorer,
tabletop, wire brush, emery
cloth, paint, batten.
The railings that you find

often tend to be in poor
condition. You will have to
strip them with the wire
brush and emery cloth, and
then paint them. This style
of plain and graphic railing
is more suitable than
railings with complicated
motifs. The console is fixed
to the wall on a batten into
which you will screw your
console top.

FRAMES

FRAMES, PAGES 94 TO 103

Supplies:
Drawing paper, wood glue,
cloth.
For the reproductions

used on pages 94 to 103,
the following technique
was used.
For the reproductions, black
and white drawings,
have been photocopied
onto drawing paper.
The color pictures are
color photocopies glued
using wood glue diluted
with half as much water.
Spread this preparation
on the back of the
photocopy and on the
canvas, glue them together
and with a clean rag,
dab them firmly and
hold for several minutes
so the texture of the
canvas comes through
onto the paper.

**PICTURE FRAME FOR SEVERAL
IMAGES, PAGE 94**

Supplies:
Fir wood slats, small nails,
simple bevelled molding,
velvet stretch tapes.
Cut the fir slats to the
height of the frame desired
and as many as you need
for the width. Place them
side by side with a very

narrow space between each one. Then nail a simple bevelled molding all around. Cut lengths of velvet stretch tape then nail the ends horizontally and vertically on the slats. Insert the photos.

NATURAL BEECH FRAME, PAGE 96
Supplies:
A 2-3-in. deep box, 1 wooden block the depth of the box, wooden panel, glue.
This is a four-stage operation.
1. Make a box, without a lid, the size you require, and deep enough to stand on its own.

2. Cut a wood block the same depth as the box and screw it in the middle.
3. Cut out a wooden panel which will act as the backing for the drawing, then screw it onto the block.
4. Apply photo or reproduction of your choice onto the wooden panel with wood glue.

HORIZONTAL FRAME, PAGE 96
Supplies:
2 round wooden rods, 12 non-reflecting pieces of glass, 2 lengths of wire.
In each rod make a very shallow notch running the entire length of a width equivalent to the thickness of two sheets of glass. Slip the pieces of glass, two by two, into the notch, after inserting a photo between them. Pass the wire through each end of the rods.

TORTOISESHELL-LIKE FRAME, PAGE 101
Supplies:
A 1-in. thick wood panel of wood, tortoiseshell paper, 1 sheet of aluminum.
Cut the wooden panel to the size you require. Glue the tortoiseshell paper to it. Lengthwise, in a sheet of aluminum cut out 2-in. wide strips. Nail them around the wooden panel (1 in. on the front, 1 in. on the side and back), then make a small frame in the same way, but replace the paper with a drawing, screw it to the middle of the larger frame.

SILVER FRAME, PAGE 103

Supplies:
3 sheets of silver cardboard, royal format (20 x 26 in.), 2 sheets with corrugated designs and 1 with striped designs, 1 wooden frame 11 x 9 x 2-in. wide.

In the cardboard cut 4 inner frames of 11 x 9 in. Remove the centers leaving respective widths of 2 in., 3 in., 3 1/2 in. and 4 in. Overlay and glue the inner frames starting by the opening of the smallest one and finishing with the largest. Then glue the whole thing to the wooden frame. In the largest remaining sheet, cut two strips of 9 x 1 in. and two strips of 11 x 1 in., and glue them to the thickness of the frame obtained.

SILVER FRAME, GRAY AND WHITE, PAGE 103

Supplies:
3 sheets of corrugated cardboard, royal format (20 x 26 in.): 1 white, 1 silver, 1 gray; 1 wooden frame 9 x 11 x 1 1/2-in. wide. 1 balsa wood rod, 1/2 in. section x 16-in. long.

In the gray board cut out an inner frame of 9 x 11 in., remove the center leaving a width of 3 in. and cut the corners diagonally. In the silver cardboard of 9 x 11 in., cut out a 3 1/2 in. inner frame. In the white cardboard make two inner frames of 9 x 11 in., leaving a width of 3 1/2 in. for one and just under 4 in. for the other. Overlay and glue the three white and silver inner frames from the opening of the smallest to the largest and fix them to the wooden frame. Turn this over and place the gray inner frame on the edge of the silver inner frame. Glue 4 4 in. balsa wood rods so that the edges of the gray inner frame are raised.

Useful Addresses

FURNITURE AND ACCESSORIES

ABC CARPET & HOME
(ACCESSORIES, ARTIFACTS, FURNITURE, REPRODUCTIONS)
www.abchome.com
P: 212-473-3000

BAKER FURNITURE
(TRADITIONAL FURNITURE, REPRODUCTIONS)
www.bakerfurnitue.com
P: 800-59-BAKER
P: 860-684-2256
(reproductions information)

BRITISH KHAKI
(HANDCRAFTED FURNITURE)
www.britishkhaki.com
P: 212-343-2299

CASSINA
(CONTEMPORARY DESIGN FURNITURE)
www.cassinausa.com
P: 800-770-3568

CENTURY
(TRADITIONAL FURNITURE, UPHOLSTERY COLLECTIONS)
www.centuryfurniture.com
P: 800-852-5552

THE CONRAN SHOP
(ACCESSORIES, DESIGN FURNITURE, LIGHTING)
www.conran.com
P: 866-755-9079

CRATE & BARREL
(ACCESSORIES, FURNITURE, LIGHTING, TEXTILES, WINDOW TREATMENTS)
www.crateandbarrel.com
P: 800-967-6696

DENNIS MILLER ASSOCIATES
(DESIGN CHAIRS, TABLES)
www.dennismiller.com
P: 212-684-0070

DONGHIA
(DESIGN FURNITURE, TEXTILES, UPHOLSTERY, WICKER AND RATTAN, TABLES)
www.donghia.com
P: 800-366-4442

ETHAN ALLEN
(CUSTOM DRAPERY, HOME FURNISHINGS, LIGHTING)
www.ethanallen.com
P: 888-EA-HELP1

GRANGE
(CABINETRY, ARMCHAIRS, SOFAS, SOLID WOOD FURNITURE)
www.grange.fr
P: 800-GRANGE-1

GUMPS
(ACCESSORIES, FURNITURE, RUGS)
www.gumps.com
P: 800-436-4311

HENREDON
(CLASSIC AND EUROPEAN FURNITURE, UPHOLSTERY)
www.henredon.com
P: 800-444-3682

HICKORY CHAIR
(CLASSIC FURNITURE)
www.hickorychair.com
P: 828-324-1801

IKEA
(ACCESSORIES, FURNITURE, LIGHTING, RUGS)
www.ikea-usa.com

KNOLL
(DESIGN CHAIRS, TABLES)
www.knoll.com
P: 800-343-5665

LAFCO
(CONTEMPORARY FURNITURE,
ACCESSORIES)
www.lafcony.com
P: 800-362-3677

LES MIGRATEURS
(FURNITURE, UPHOLSTERY)
www.lesmigrateurs.com
P: 207-846-1430

LINDA HORN
(ANTIQUES)
www.lindahorn.com
P: 800-772-8008

MOLTENI
(CONTEMPORARY FURNITURE)
www.molteni.it
P: 201-585-9420

OLY
(HANDCRAFTED FURNITURE,
UPHOLSTERY, ACCESSORIES)
www.olystudio.com
P: 510-644-1870

PIER 1 IMPORTS
(ACCESSORIES, FURNITURE,
WINDOW TREATMENTS)
www.pier1.com
P: 800-245-4595

PIERCE MARTIN
(WICKER, RATTAN AND IRON
FURNISHINGS, ASIAN
ANTIQUES, ACCESSORIES)
www.piercemartin.com
P: 800-334-8701

POLIFORM USA
(CONTEMPORARY FURNITURE)
www.poliformusa.com
P: 888-POLIFORM

PUCCI
(CONTEMPORARY FURNITURE)
www.ralphpucci.com
P: 212-633-0452

REPERTOIRE
(CONTEMPORARY FURNITURE)
www.repertoire.com
P: 212-219-8159

RESTORATION HARDWARE
(ACCESSORIES, FURNITURE,
WINDOW TREATMENTS)
www.restorationhardware.com
P: 800-762-1005

ROCHE BOBOIS
(PERIOD AND STYLE FURNITURE)
www.roche-bobois.com
P: 800-972-8375

STOREHOUSE
(FURNITURE, UPHOLSTERY)
www.storehouse.com
P: 888-STOREHOUSE

FABRICS

BERGAMO
(LUXURY FABRICS)
www.bergamofabrics.com
P: 914-665-0800

BOUSSAC
(LUXURY FABRICS)
www.boussac-fadini.fr
P: 866-268-7722

BRUNSCHWIG & FILS
(FABRICS, HOME
FURNISHINGS, LAMPS)
www.brunschwig.com

F. SCHUMACHER & CO.
(FABRICS, HOME FASHIONS,
WALLPAPER)
www.fschumacher.com
P: 800-332-3384

J. ROBERT SCOTT
(TEXTILES, ACCESSORIES)
www.jrobertscott.com
P: 800-322-4910

KRAVET
(FABRICS, TRIMMINGS)
www.kravet.com
P: 800-648-KRAV

PIERRE FREY
(LUXURY FABRICS)
www.pierrefrey.com
P: 212-213-3099

WAVERLY
(FABRICS, WALLPAPER)
www.waverly.com
P: 800-423-5881

CARPETS AND RUGS

ABC CARPET & HOME
(LUXURY CARPETS, FABRICS)
www.abchome.com
P: 212-473-3000

CAPEL
(AREA RUGS)
www.capelrugs.com
P: 800-382-6574

CALVIN KLEIN
(AREA RUGS)
P: 800-294-7978

COURISTAN
(HANDMADE AND
BROADLOOM RUGS)
www.couristan.com
P: 800-223-6186

ENDLESS KNOT
(CLASSIC, CONTEMPORARY,
TIBETAN RUGS)
www.endlessknotrugs.com
P: 800-910-3000

HABIDECOR
(LUXURY RUGS)
www.habidecorusa.com
P: 800-588-8565

KARASTAN
(LUXURY CARPETS AND RUGS)
www.karastan.com
P: 800-234-1120

**M & M DESIGN
INTERNATIONAL**
(ORIENTAL AND
CUSTOM RUGS)
www.mandmgallery.com
P: 516-456-0681

**MICHAEL AZIZ
ORIENTAL RUGS**
(PAKISTAN RUGS)
www.michaelazizrugs.com
P: 212-686-8755

NOURISON
(HANDMADE RUGS)
www.nourison.com
P: 800-223-1110

ODEGARD
(LUXURY CARPETS)
www.odegardinc.com
P: 800-670-8836

TILES

AMTICO
(CERAMIC, GLASS,
GRANITE, MARBLE, SHELL,
MOSAICS, STONE)
www.amtico.com
P: 800-268-4260

ANN SACKS
(CERAMIC, GLASS, MOSAICS,
PORCELAIN, STONE)
www.annsacks.com
P: 800-278-8453

ARTISTIC TILE
(CERAMIC, GLASS, MOSAICS,
PORCELAIN, STONE)
www.artistictile.com
P: 800-260-8646

BISAZZA
(GLASS, MOSAICS)
www.bisazzausa.com

COUNTRY FLOORS
(MOSAICS, TERRA COTTA)
www.countryfloors.com
P: 800-311-9995

DUPONT
(TILING)
www.corian.com
P: 800-4-CORIAN

EMAUX DE BRIARE
(TILING)
www.emauxdebriare.com
P: 516-931-5924

HASTINGS TILE
(GLASS, MOSAICS,
PORCELAIN, STONE)
www.hastingstilebath.com
P: 516-379-3500

PARIS CERAMICS
(DECORATIVE CERAMIC,
ANTIQUE TERRA COTTA,
MOSAICS)
www.parisceramics.com
P: 888-845-3487

WALKER ZANGER
(CERAMIC, GLASS, METAL,
STONE, TERRA COTTA)
www.walkerzanger.com
P: 877-611-0199

LIGHTING SPECIALISTS

ROBERT ABBEY
(LIGHTING DESIGN)
www.robertabbey.com
P: 828-322-3480

ARTEMIDE
(LIGHTING DESIGN)
www.artemide.com
P: 631-694-9292

CX DESIGN
(LIGHTING DESIGN)
P: 888-431-4242

FLOS
(LIGHTING DESIGN)
www.flos.net
P: 800-939-3567

NAMBE
(LIGHTING DESIGN,
ACCESSORIES)
www.nambe.com
P: 800-443-0339

JAMIE YOUNG
(LIGHTING DESIGN,
ACCESSORIES)
www.jamieyoung.com
P: 888-671-5883

DO-IT-YOURSELF MATERIALS

EXPO DESIGN CENTER
(DECORATIVE ACCESSORIES,
LIGHTING, HARDWARE)
www.expo.com
P: 800-350-1481

HOME DEPOT
(PAINT, DECOR, FLOORING
HARDWARE, TOOLS)
www.homedepot.com
P: 800-430-3376

RENOVATOR'S SUPPLY
(FIXTURES, LIGHTING,
HARDWARE)
www.rensup.com
P: 800-659-2211

Credits

Curtains. P. 8: Curtains fabric, "Anatole" Deschemecker. Organdi, Marie Gouny. Rod, Houlè Armchair, "Malacca," Habitat. Drapes "Blanc d'Ivoire," Pierre Frey. P. 10-11: Curtains made b Brigitte Lefort. Ribbons, Mokuba. P. 12-13: Curtains made by Brigitte Lefort. Fabric "Cotton Club. Manuel Canovas. Rods, The Conran Shop.

Tiebacks. P. 14: Table, vase and bowl, Modénature. Fabric, Manuel Canovas. P. 15: Curtains, Thor P. 16-17: Curtains fabric, Manuel Canovas.

Shades. P. 18: Shades, D'Artigny de Romanex. Soft furnishings striped fabric, Thorp. P. 20-2 Blinds, Les Ateliers du Petit Cerf for Les Labradors Décorateurs. Flowers, Marianne for Lilia François. Lampshade, Clair-Obscur. P. 22-23: Fabric shades, Rubelli. P. 24: Shade made by Brigitt Lefort, fabric "Les Portes" 100% linen, Bisson Bruneel. P. 25: Shade made by Brigitte Lefort, fabric "Chine" and "Les Portes," Bisson Bruneel. P. 26-27: Shades, Belzacq. Rug, Château Frères. P. 2 Shade, Modo France. Shade "Riloga," Bon Marché. Shade, Habitat. P. 29: Shade, Franciaflex wit Baumann fabric. Shade "Soleil levant" by Marie-Thérèse Lemoine, Eurodrap.

Lampshades. P. 30: Wooden candlestick holders "Torsade" and "Vrille," Siècle. Candles, Point à Ligne. Flowerpot, Mise en Demeure. Wooden frame, Siècle. Flowers, Christian Tortu. Excerpt fro Amelia Saint-George's book. P. 32: Candlestick holders, Mise en Demeure. Blown crystal pitche "Darabella." Candlestick holder, Boutique du Musée des Arts Décoratifs. Buttonholes, Mathias. Candl and candlestick holders, Point à la ligne. P. 33: Right: Candlestick holders, Wegwood. Left: candlestic holder, Véronique Pichon Terre de Sienne. Candles, Point à la ligne. Plates, Boutique du Musée des Ar Décoratifs. Jar and braided bowl, Véronique Pichon Terre de Sienne. Ribbons, Mokuba. P. 35, left t right, top to bottom: 1. Lace lampshade, Semaine. 2. Pearls lampshade, Magnum. 3. Ted co lampshade, The Conran Shop. 4. Hearts lampshade "Leedsware," Laura Ashley. 5. Yellow lampshad The Conran Shop. 6. White lampshade, Habitat. 7. Yellow lampshade, "Tamaris" Madura. 8. Yello with red and gold lampshade "Colonial" Point à la ligne. 9. Red, orange and yellow scallope lampshades, Le Bon Marché. 10. Stars lampshade, Le Bon Marché.

Paint. P. 36: Satin finish wood paint, Astral. Varnish, Astral. Armchair and quilted blanket, Fanett Hat box, Louis Vuitton. P 37: Accessories, BHV. P. 38-39: Paint, Tollens. P. 40-41: Satin finis lacquer, "Valénite" by Valentine. Varnish, Valentine. Paintings, Jacques Leguennec. Chair, Mise e Demeure. Armchair, pillows and boxes, Habitat. Hat "Claudette," Toute la Terre. Pillows on the floo Les Bugadières. P. 42: Matte acrylic paint, Valentine. Lamp, Yves Halard. Armchair and pots, Mise e Demeure. Floors and rugs, Crucial Trading. Médicis vase, Christian Tortu. Doorknob, Brass. P. 4: Matte and satin paint, Astral. "Rebecca" table and "Lucas" stool, Yves Halard. "Nessim," Julie Prisc ug. Crucial Trading. Doorknob, Brass. Flowers, Marianne Robic. P. 44-45: Satin paint, Avi 3000. rmchair, Le Cèdre rouge. Pillows, Habitat. Flowerpot, Fanette. Candles, Le Grand Magasin. Basket, ise en Demeure. Lamp, candlestick holders and table, Yves Halard. Fireplace screen, shovel set and re iron, Le Salon B. Rug, Agnès Comar.

urniture to paint. P. 46: Paint, Avi, Valentine, Ripolin, Astral, Sikkens. Brushes and fabric, BHV. 47: Drawer handles, Siècle. P. 48: Basque-red paint, Astral Gel. Salad spinner, kitchen utensils, oil ottle, vase, pitcher and glasses, The Conran Shop. Dishcloths, Le Jacquard Français at Maison de amille. Wine rack, Etamine. Painting and basket, Habitat. Basket, Maison de Famille. P. 49: Moss reen paint, Avi Satin 3000. Shawl Etamine. Frames, Hilton McConnico. Fabric, BHV. P. 50: Pearl-gray nd white paint, Valentine. Lamp, Maison de Famille. Perfume bottle, Eau de Saint-Louis. Soap holder nd faucet, L'Épi d'Or. Bottle and jewels, Lalique. Eau de toilette, Equipage Hermès. Perfume, litsouko Guerlain, L'Eau d'Issey Miyaké. Bottle, Maison de Famille. Eau de Cologne Impérial uerlain. White towel, Catherine Memmi. Black towel, Living Tradition. Sink, Idéal Standard. P. 51: lue paint, Avi. White paint, Ripolin 500.

lipcovers. P. 52: Blankets, La Tranchée Militaire. Braid, Mokuba. P. 53: Fabric "Les Chevrons," ominique Kieffer, Les Impressions Edition. P. 54: Fabric "Bizone," Edmond Petit. P. 55: Fabric Cancale," Toile de Mayenne. P. 56-57: Rod, BHV. Fabric "Roselyne," Yves Halard for Lauer. Mattress Bi-portance," Dunlopillo. P. 58: Fabric "Le lin," les Impressions for Etamine. Mattress and eadboards, "Mérinos," Exigence. P. 59: Fabric "Les Toiles Coton," Eurodif and Bouchara. Mattress Multispire," Épeda. Pillows, Plume Industrie. P. 60: Fabric "Cotton Stripe," Jane Churchill Colefax nd Flower. P. 61: Fabric Pierre Frey. Tassels, Houlès. P. 62: Fabric "Lahore," Manuel Canovas. P. 63: abric "Caldeira," Dominique Kieffer Les Impressions. P. 64: Sofa Giorgio Soresi, Nouveaux Classiques, Tosca" Roche Bobois. Footstool, Etamine. P. 65: Chairs, Haga.

eproductions. The chairs featured from pages 66 to 73 were manufactured by the Coulombs rniture factory, sold at Galerie du Bac. They were painted by Rigolot. P. 67: Chair "Legdiguières." P. 8: Armchair "Mireille." Fabric "Limousine," Canovas. P. 69: Armchair "Barnave." Fabric "Sirocco," omanex. P. 70: Chair "Necker." Fabric, Porthault. P. 71: Wing chair "Calonne." Fabric "Art oderne," Pierre Frey.

loors. P. 72: Tiles 12 x 12 in., Imola. Tiles 2 x 2 in., Winckelmans Frazzi MMM. Soap and brushes, rain de beauté. Sponge, Bon Marché. P. 74: Tiles 4 x 4 in., Winckelmans. Tiles 1 x 1 in., Cérabati razzi MMM. Dish, Kitchen Bazaar Autrement. P. 75: Tiles 12 x 12 in., Imola. Tiles 2 x 2 in., Vinckelmans Frazzi MMM. P. 76, from left to right, top to bottom: Rug "Sudbury," collection "Stripes," he Hartley Collection. Rug "Elysée," Manufacture Royale du Parc. Rug "Galon," Manufacture Royale u Parc. Rug "Chevrons," collection "Stripes," The Hartley Collection. P. 77, from left to right, top to ottom: Rug "Bellagio," D. Filé. Rug "Malton," collection "Stripes," The Hartley Collection. Rug

"Wilton," Tapis et Moquettes de France. Rug "Malton," collection "Stripes," The Hartley Collection. Rug "Chevrons," Crucial Trading. P. 78-79, left to right: Rug, Codimat. Rug, Etamine, "Épinglés," Osborne and Little. Border, Houlès. Rug, David Hicks.

Screens. P. 80: White and ecru paper strips, Le Bon Marché. Vase, pillow, soap, scarf, Côté Bastide. P. 81: Wool and knitting accessories, La Droguerie. Boxes, Habitat. P. 82: Chairs, Siège Vieille France. Wooden boxes, Espace Cordon. Lamp, Rougier & Plé. Stars, Atelier Sedap. P. 83: Chair and armchair, Marway. Fabric, Pierre Frey. P. 84: Sofa, Yves Halard. Tea set, Allure. P. 85: Bench, Keroll International. Lamp, Alain Demachy for Galerie Camoin.

Tabletops and legs. P. 86-87: Tabletops found in flea markets. Legs, Godin. Dishes and vases, Quartz. Glasses, candlestick holders, plates, Yves Halard. Pitcher, Forestier. Flowers, Fleurs. Floor, Galerie Farnese. P. 88-89, from left to right: Table Directoire, Toury. Flowers, Des Fleurs. Floor, Galerie Farnese. Washstand, Le Bain Rose. Vinegar and oil bottles, jam and fruit, olive oil can, Kitchen Bazaar Autrement. White iron cake pans, Dehillerin. Floor, Galerie Farnese. Pedestal sink, Le Bain Rose. Flower holder, Le Cèdre Rouge. Floor, Galerie Farnese. P. 90: Tiles 12 x 12 in., Carrelages du Marais. Vase, Le Cèdre rouge. Wrought-iron stand, Jan Firch, Marché Serpette. P. 91: Vase, Textures. P. 92: Tiles 4 x 4 in. and frieze tiles, Mosaïque Noir d'Ivoire. P. 93: Tiles, Carrelages du Marais. Vase, Le Cèdre Rouge.

Frames and stands. P. 94: Ribbon, Mokuba. P. 98: Velvet, Saint-Honoré by Pierre Frey. Black wood, Brio. P. 99: Black folded paper, Calligrane. P. 100: Oval frame, La Baguette de Bois. Natural linen, La Baguette de Bois. P. 101: Tortoiseshell-patterned paper, Calligrane. P. 103: Cardboard, Le Bon Marché. Glass, book, Côté Bastide. P. 104: Leather bracelet "Le Homard" and armchair, Christian Astuguevieille. Lock, Bambara. Statues, Ibeji. Statue, Senoufo. P. 106: Whitewashed wooden frames, Cadre Espace. Tiger balm and sari blouses, Sarre Housse. American-Indian headdress and squaw doll, Galerie Urubamba. Seashells, Galerie Laquaris. Beetles "Hippopotame," RMN. Mao badges, CFOC. Table, Yves Halard. Lamps and vases, Modénature. P. 107: Black frames, The Conran Shop. Champagne, Krug. Table, plates, vinegar, oil and artichokes, Habitat. P. 108: Art, Charles Matton. Stand, Atelier Christian de Beaumont. Woodwork, Joël Féau. Carpets, Casa Lopez. P. 109, from left to right: Art "Seated Woman," Philippe Anthonioz. P. 110: Tri-footed bronze stand, present from Sarah Moon to Charles Matton. Woodwork, Joël Féau. Painting, Boutique du Louvre or boutique du Forum des Halles. Wooden column, Atelier Christian de Beaumont. Plaster bust, Philippe Anthonioz. Tripod, Atelier Christian de Beaumont. Light, Cohérence. Tripod in bronze, Atelier de Beaumont.

The publisher wishes to thank the Elle Studio: Michel Bouveau, Jean-Pierre Naivin, Eddy Kauffmann.

Photographs:

Fabrice Bouquet: p. 28
Robert Demachy: p. 97 (bottom)
Jacques Dirand: p. 104, 105
Alain Gelberger: p. 14, 34, 35, 76, 77
Daniel Jouanneau: p. 66, 67, 68, 69, 70, 71
Joël Laiter: p. 52, 53, 54, 55
Guillaume de Laubier: p. 18, 19, 20, 21, 22, 23, 26, 27, 29, 64, 65, 83
Guillaume de Laubier, Marianne Haas, Alexandre Bailhache: p. 16 (top)
Didier Massard: p. 108, 109, 110, 111
Patrice Pascal: p. 8, 9, 10, 11, 12, 13, 15, 16 (bottom), 17, 30, 31, 32, 33, 36, 37, 38, 39, 40, 41, 42, 43, 44, 45, 46, 47, 48, 49, 50, 51, 56, 57, 58, 59, 60, 61, 62, 63, 72, 73, 74, 75, 78, 79, 81, 84, 85, 86, 87, 88, 89, 90, 91, 92, 93, 94, 95, 96, 97, 98, 99, 100, 101, 102, 106, 107
Edouard Sicot: p. 82
Gilles Trillard: p. 80, 103
Yutaka Yamamoto: p. 24, 25

Words and style:

Marie-Claire Blanckaert: p. 16 (top), 18, 19, 20, 21, 22, 23, 26, 27, 29, 65, 83
Barbara Bourgois: p. 8, 9, 10, 11, 12, 13, 15, 16 (bottom), 24, 25, 30, 31, 32, 33, 34, 35, 36, 37, 38, 39, 40, 41, 42, 43, 44, 45, 46, 47, 48, 49, 50, 51, 52, 53, 54, 55, 56, 57, 58, 59, 60, 61, 62, 63, 66, 67, 68, 69, 70, 71, 72, 73, 74, 75, 78, 79, 80, 81, 82, 84, 85, 86, 87, 88, 89, 90, 91, 92, 93, 95, 96, 97, 98, 99, 100, 101, 102, 103, 106, 107, 108, 109, 110, 111
Barbara Bourgois, Françoise Tournier: p. 17
Marie Kalt, Emma Bernhardt, Claire Heseltine: p. 64
Andréa Lucas-Pauwels: p. 28, 76, 77
Andréa Lucas-Pauwels, Françoise Tournier: p. 14
Gérard Pussey: p. 104, 105
Misha de Potestad: p. 94

All examples shown on pages 30 to 34 are from Amelia Saint-George's book, *Abat-jour*, Editions Armand Colin.

Elle Decor (U.S.) and *Elle Décoration* (France) are both imprints of the Hachette Filipacchi group.
The content of this book was taken solely from *Elle Décoration* and appeared only in France.

**Under the direction of
Jean Demachy**

Editorial
Barbara Bourgois

Art direction
Marie-France Fèvre-Couanault

Copy editing
Claire Cornubert
and Samantha Deplanque

Picture research
Geneviève Tartrat

Text research
Sandrine Hess